Problems and Challenges in Food Security Programme during Disasters

Problems and Challenges in Food Security Programme during Disasters

Karanam Viswa Bhushan

GYAN

Published, 2020

Published by

Gyan Publishing House
5, Ansari Road
Daryaganj, New Delhi-110002
Phone: 011-47034999, 9811692060
www.gyanbooks.com
E-mail: books@gyanbooks.com

Printed at: Gyan Press, Delhi.

Cataloging in Publication Data—DK
Courtesy: D.K. Agencies (P) Ltd. <docinfo@dkagencies.com>

Bhushan, Karanam Viswa, 1963- **author.**
Problems and challenges in food security programme during disasters / Karanam Viswa Bhushan.
pages cm
Study conducted in Dewe District, Afar Region, Ethiopia.
Includes bibliographical references.
ISBN 9788121220309 (HB)

1. Food security—Climatic factors—Ethiopia—Dewe (District) 2. Disasters—Ethiopia—Dewe (District) I. Title.

LCC HD9000.5.B48 2021 | DDC 363.80963 23

Acknowledgments

I would like to express my deepest and heartfelt gratitude to the Almighty God.

I am thankful to my student Mohammed Murha for his continuous efforts and sincere involvement for this research study.

I would like to thank whole heartedly and express my gratitude to my friend Gerd for her deep sense of inspiration and encouragement.

Finally, I would like to thank the staff members, clients of the organisation and other research participants who supported for the research work and also to all the members who wished for the book publication.

Karanam Viswa Bhushan

Contents

List of Tables and Figures

Tables

Figures

Abbreviations

CSA	Central Statistical Authority
FAO	Food and Agricultural Organisation
FCS	Food Consumption Score
FED	Food Entitlement Decline
HFIAS	Household Food Insecurity Access Scale
ILO	International Labour Organisation
DFID	Department for International Development
DRMFSS	Disaster Risk Management and Food Security Sector
MOFED	Ministry of Finance and Economic Development
USAID	United States Agency for International Development
RCSI	Reduced Coping Strategy Index
WFP	World Food Programme

1

Introduction

1.1 Background of the Study

In Sub-Saharan Africa on the whole and in Ethiopia especially, households' capacity to manage risk is especially low due to multiple stressors coupled with a poor asset base, making them particularly vulnerable to food insecurity. Vulnerability to food insecurity is defined as the risk that a household will, if currently food secure, fall below the food security threshold, or, if food insecure remain in food insecurity. Vulnerability, therefore, is a forward-looking concept and is not directly observable. The observed food insecurity status of a household can be seen as the exposit realisation of potential food security states whose probabilities are predicted ex-ante as the household's level of vulnerability. A large proportion of observed food insecurity may be transient, with movements into and out of it. In particular, the welfare status of a substantial share of the population may be just above the food security threshold, with a high probability of falling below it in the near future. Consequently, policy interventions designed to reduce vulnerability are becoming increasingly important, making it crucial to develop reliable and easily applied measures of vulnerability to enhance the targeting efficiency of such policy measures.

The gravity of food insecurity, and its many rippling effects, has led much of the development agenda to search for specific areas for intervention given limited resources and growing populations in many developing countries. Moreover, it is essential for every country continuously to monitor its food security status, in order to uncover any hidden hunger, particularly creeping food insecurity, which may not be readily noticeable. In recent years there has been increasing awareness that the analysis of food insecurity should be carried out in a dynamic context. It is essential not just to look at the current incidence of an inadequate nutritional outcome, but also to identify the individuals, households or the communities who are more at risk of suffering in the future. The main analytical concept that has been developed in order to address the issue of the future incidence of food insecurity is vulnerability analysis.

Ethiopia is one of the most food-insecure and famine affected countries. A large portion of the country's population has been affected by chronic and transitory food insecurity African Development Bank (2014). The situation of chronically food insecure people is becoming more and more severe. Food security situation in Ethiopia is highly linked to recurring food shortage and famine in the country, which are associated to recurrent drought. According to African Development Bank (2014), more than 41 percent of the Ethiopian population lives below the poverty line and above 31 million people are undernourished. By using the threshold of 2,550 kilocalories (Kcal) per adult equivalent per day, 40 percent of Ethiopian households for whom their majority reside in rural parts of the country were food insecure and undernourished Anderson *et al.,* (2015).

As pointed out by Capaldo *et al.* (2010) food security policies should be based as much on the assessment of households' current conditions as on the expectation of their future access to food.

So as to reduce the hazard of future under nutrition, policy design should address the uncertainty that households face alongside their risk management options. Quite the reverse to this common sense, however, widely used food security analyses mainly consider present access to food. Therefore, this study will assess Food Security Programme during Disaster and its Problems and Challenges in the case of Afar Region, Dewe district, Ethiopia.

Ethiopia is chronically affected by multiple hazards as well as floods and drought as the main risks. Due to this, above 20 million people were vulnerable to poverty and food insecure. Afar, SNNPR, Somali, Amhara, Oromia and Tigray were mostly vulnerable to drought. The current frequency of drought is about every 2-3 years. The latest El Niño-affected drought, which began in 2015, is reported to be one of the most severe to have occurred during the past 30 years, affecting at least 10.2 million people in addition to the 8 million people receiving support under the on-going Productive Safety Net Programme (PSNP) ; the effects are still on-going. A second shock, from that occurred during the latter part of 2016 and into mid-2017 affected a smaller part of the country with flooding and some drought-like conditions (Dibaba, 2018).

1.2 Statement of the Problem

It is well thought-out that over 854 million people in the world are affected by food insecurity from which - according to assessments made by the Food and Agriculture Organisation of the United Nations (FAO) in the years 2001/2003- 820 million are in developing countries, 25 million in countries in transition and 9 million in industrialised countries (FAO, 2006). A common strategy among different nations of the world to reduce or eliminate all manifestations of hunger and tackle food insecurity is currently under implementation as the World Food Summit and the Millennium Development Goals have proposed, i.e., to achieve the halving in the proportion of people in the world who suffer from hunger. The time horizon raised for the achievement of this goal is the year 2015, focusing on developing countries to generate food plans, national and regional Programmes, and public policies aimed at improving the food security.

With a population projected to reach 80 million in 2010 and about 45 percent living below the poverty line and most vulnerable to food insecurity, ensuring food security remained a key issue for the Government of Ethiopia (MoFED, 2002).

In order to combat threats of famine and pervasive poverty and thereby ensure food security for its population, the government strategy has rested on increasing the availability of foodgrains through significant investments in agricultural technologies (high yielding varieties of seeds, fertiliser), services (extension, credit, inputs), and rural infrastructure (roads, markets). The impacts of these policies, however, have been shadowed as there are still millions of people who experience extreme hunger in the country

(Bogale & Shimalis, 2009). Moreover, the achievement of food self-sufficiency is one of the key objectives of the government as articulated in its GTP and rural development policies and strategies, which is also consistent with the MDG goal of eradicating extreme poverty or hunger (MoFED, 2012). Mainly this is due to access to sufficient food and nutrients are essential for household welfare, as well as for accomplishing other development objectives. Households within sufficient access to food often face other challenges related to food insecurity including poor health and a decline in productivity. These challenges can often create a vicious circle whereby households are unable to produce enough food, even in good years, because they are battling chronic health issues and are unable to work to their full potential. Many scholars conducted different studies on food security and its challenges but in Afar region especially, Dewe district it is less considered. Cognizant of this fact, this study, attempted to fill the gap by assessing Food Security Programme during Disaster and its Problems and Challenges in the case of Afar Region, Dewe district, Ethiopia.

1.3 Research Objective

1.3.1 General Objective

The main objective of the study is to assess Food Security Programme during Disaster and its Problems and Challenges in the case of Afar Region, Dewe district, Ethiopia.

1.3.2 Specific Objectives

- To assess how disasters affect food security in the case of Afar Region, Dewe district, Ethiopia.
- To profile the level of household food insecurity in the study areas.
- To estimate the vulnerability to food insecurity of households quantitatively.
- To identify who is vulnerable to food insecurity and analyse the socio-economic characteristics of households with higher vulnerability.

- To identify the challenges influencing food security in the case of Afar Region, Dewe district, Ethiopia.

1.4 Research Questions

- How disasters affect food security in the case of Afar Region, Dewe district, Ethiopia?
- What is the current rate of food insecurity in the research area?
- Who is vulnerable to food insecurity and what are the characteristics of households with vulnerability?
- Do the households with vulnerability differ from characteristics featuring households with food insecurity?
- What are the challenges influencing food security in the case of Afar Region, Dewe district, Ethiopia?

1.5 Significance of the Study

Food security and vulnerability analysis enabled us to identify the food secure and insecure households within communities and try to predict how the different segments of population will be affected by unexpected adverse events. Such an identification mechanism can be used to design appropriate pre-and post-shock institutional assistance strategies. Aid agencies and development organisations continue to face challenges of needs assessment and targeting interventions since there is a lack of mechanisms that can be used to differentiate food secure from food insecure or at-risk households. Therefore, it becomes important to identify the food insecure sections of the society and predict how their situation be when they face an adverse shock. Once the insecure or at-risk households are identified and we know what resources they lack, interventions can be designed to provide the households with those resources, thus enabling them to get out of hunger trap.

Moreover, a deeper understanding of the characteristics of vulnerable groups would provide an emphirical basis for social policy, thereby strengthening both the analytical and operational content of Ethiopian poverty reduction programme in general and the study area in particular. This study therefore provide an approach on what can be done to help the current food insecure to be food secure and to reduce the likelihood of the vulnerable from falling into food insecurity in the future. Consequently, such studies are away from doubt important for the success of efforts to be made in the area to ensure food security. Policy makers and planners will also draw lessons on designing effective strategies to reduce not only current food inadequacy faced by households but also exposure to future food insecurity.

1.6 Scope and Limitations of the Study

This study was limited toDewe district of Afar Region, Ethiopia. It aimed to assess Food Security Programme during Disaster and its Problems and Challenges in the case of Afar Region, Dewe district, Ethiopia. Various studies of Ethiopian household livelihood and coping strategies have found that household members may not fully share risk factors for undernutrition, and an individual in a household that is defined as not being undernourished, may be in fact undernourished (Dercon and Krishnan, 2000). Given data constraints, the researcher was unable to calculate calorie intake variations within the household.

1.7 Organisation of the Study

This study manuscript comprised of five main chapters. The first chapter presents introduction of the study that incorporates background of the study statement of the problem, objectives and research questions, significance, scope and limitations of the study. Chapter two, review of literature, illustrates the concepts as well as the theoretical and empirical basis of the study. Chapter three presents the setting, materials and methods used in the study. Chapter four contains data analysis and presentation while chapter five contains summary, conclusion and recommendation.

2

Literature Review

Introduction

This chapter contains different conceptual, theoretical, and empirical studies regarding the study area. Different studies at International, African and Ethiopian level will be discussed.

2.1 Concepts and Theories of Food Security

2.1.1 The Concept of Food Security

Over the years, several definitions have been forwarded to the concept of food security. Smith *et al.* (1992), for instance, have documented about 194 definitions of food security. However, the definition that appears in FAO (2000) is generally considered as more comprehensive one. FAO (2000) conceptualises food security as a situation that occurs when "all people, at all times, have physical, social, and economic access to sufficient, safe and nutritious food which meets their dietary needs and food preferences for an active and healthy life". According to Devereux (2004), the opposite of food security is food insecurity and hence people who do not satisfy the conditions in this definition are considered food insecure. Degefa (2005) underlines the importance of people's own perception in food security/insecurity definition and defines food insecurity, at household level, as the fear of being unable to sufficiently feed household members all year round. According to the Degefa (2005), such fear emerges from various situations of a household such as lack of information, past experiences in relation to hazards, social position in a society, and current circumstances. This way of conceptualising food insecurity/security too is not at odds with the FAO's definition mentioned here except its emphasis on the importance of subjective views and evaluation of households about their own food security status when it comes to assessment.

Cognizant of the FAO's definition, literatures such as Gross *et al.* (2000) and Barrett (2010) and Sasi (2015) in Dula and Degefa (2017) identify four dimensions or components of food security: availability, access, utilisation, and stability. According to Gross *et al.* (2000), availability is achieved if adequate food is ready to have at people's disposal. It refers to the physical existence of food, whether from the household's own production or from markets: domestic or international. Hoddinott and Yisehac (2002) consider availability as a measure of food that is, and will be, physically available in the relevant vicinity of a population during a given period.

According to USAID (1992) and Goitom (2017), the availability requirement is met when sufficient quantities of appropriate and necessary types of food are consistently available either from domestic production, commercial imports, aid Programmes, or food stocks to individuals.

LIFT and USAID (2011) discusses the utilisation component of food security by relating to the actual food that is consumed by individuals; how it is stored, prepared, and consumed; and what nutritional benefits the individual derives from consumption. According to LIFT and USAID (2011), food utilisation has both a socio-economic dimension - decisions related to what food is consumed and how the food is allocated within the household and biological dimension- the ability of the human body to take food and transform it into energy for daily activities or to store it for future energy needs. Gross *et al.* (2000) also link utilisation with the ability of the human body to ingest and metabolise food considering nutritious and safe diets, an adequate biological and social environment, a proper healthcare to avoid diseases as basic to ensure adequate utilisation of food. Nutrient losses due to factors like knowledge gap in food preparation, nutrition, childcare, and sanitation as well as cultural practices that limit consumption of an nutritionally adequate diet by certain groups or family members are deemed to be constraints to adequate utilisation of food (USAID, 1992).

The fourth component of the food security implicated in the definition, which means stability, cuts across the other three components. It refers to the temporal dimension, or time-frame, of food security as implied by the phrase *"at all times"* in the above definition. Insights from the stability dimension of food security have brought the convention of seeing food insecurity in terms of transitory and chronic perspectives (World Bank, 1986 and Reutlinger, 1987 in Alem, 2007, Maxwell and Smith, 1992, LIFT and USAID, 2011, Degefa, 2001). According to the resources, chronic food insecurity refers to the continuous/or persistent inability to meet food needs, while transitory food insecurity is a short-term food shortfall. Also there is a tendency to divide transitory food security in to two sub-classes: cyclical food insecurity and temporary food insecurity (CIDA, 1989 in Meseret, 2013). Cyclical (seasonal) food insecurity occurs periodically more or less on a predictable basis such as the 'lean season' that occurs in the period just before the harvest. Temporary food insecurity occurs for a short duration due to unforeseen and unpredictable conditions. Though conceptualised as distinct, the two types of food security are closely related as one has the potential of inducing the other. For instance, successively occurring transitory food insecurity or stress can increase households/individuals vulnerability to chronic food insecurity by making them to erode their assets to cope with such stress (Maxwell and Smith, 1992).

2.1.2. Food Security Theories

With the advancement of the food security concept/issue to the mainstream development agenda, there comes various theories or approaches that provides explanation on different aspects of it such as how and at what level should its analysis, measurement and focus be. As argued in Burchi and De Muro (2012) this, the way food security is theorised, measured, and finally analysed, is important as it affects the typology of policies to be adopted. Some of these theories of food security have been briefly discussed below.

2.1.3 Food Availability Decline

Food Availability Decline (FAD) is considered as the oldest and still functional theory whose origin is, arguably, traced back to

Thomas Malthus's work of 1789. As it goes in Malthusian tradition, the focus of this theory is on the disequilibrium between population and food and argues that in order to maintain the equilibrium, the rate of growth of food availability should not be lower than the rate of growth of population (Burchi and De Muro, 2012).

However, Degefa (2005) disaggregates the FAD theory into two set of theories: climatic theories that links food shortages with natural calamities such as flood and draught and demographic theories that focuses on the nexus between food availability and population growth. The climatic theories link food insecurity with such natural causes like drought and flood. According to Degefa (2005), climatic variables can lead to famine, specially, in rain-fed agricultural areas by causing crop failure, as well as, by adversely affecting other assets of livelihood among subsistence farmers.

Degefa (2005) points out the existence of two divergent and competing theories regarding the relationship between population growth and food availability. The first one focuses on comparing the relative pace at which population and food or means of subsistence increases and argues that while population grows 'geometrically', production and means of subsistence increase only 'arithmetically' with the clear outcome of such imbalance is inducing hunger and other forms of human poverty and misery. This outlook falls in the line of Malthusian thinking and a bit criticised by writers like Devereux (1993) in Degefa (2005) for its failure to foresee the mediation effect of technological improvements such as production, distribution, and communication technologies. This, the claimed, loophole of the Malthusian theory has given impetus for the emergence of alternative views regarding the population and food availability linkage: the Marxist line of thinking that associates food insecurity with the structure of society and the theory of Ester Boserup that argues for the positive effect of population on agricultural production. As indicated in Degefa (2005), Boserup (1965) sees population growth as a force leading to adoption and diffusion of technological innovation that expands agricultural production, thereby reducing vulnerability to food insecurity and hunger. As they stand at opposite poles, the Malthusian and Boserupian line of thinking may lead to different policy suggestions when it comes to the questions of which side of the food equation, supply or demand, the focus of the food security ensuring effort be.

Though there exist such divergent views under it, food security in the context of FAD theory in general is a matter of aggregate or per capita food availability (Alamgir, 1980 in Degefa, 2001, Burchi and De Muro, 2012) and the focus is merely on food production or supply side variables.

2.1.3.1 Income Based Approach

Income-based approach emerged as a critique to FAD whose focus is, as claimed, narrowly on the agricultural production. The FAD approach has been criticised for losing a sight about the interdependent nature of various sectors of the economy and viewing food insecurity as the problem of agricultural sector/production alone (Burchi and De Muro, 2012). In effect, the income based approach broadens the analysis of food security by shifting the attention to national economies as a whole and by bringing into the analysis such variables as Gross Domestic Product (GDP) and economic growth.

Moreover, it has brought a shift from food availability at macro-level to income at micro-level.

Here, food insecurity is implicitly assumed as a sub-category of poverty, often referred to as "food poverty", representing lack of enough income necessary to buy at the given conditions the amount of food required. In particular, the different food items are converted into calories and if people's calorie availability is lower than a threshold identified by international nutritionists, they are considered food insecure (Sibrian *et al.*, 2007 and Sibrian, 2008 both cited in Burchi and De Muro, 2012). With this, the level of analysis of food security is stretched down to the individual and/or household level with income and expenditure approach being a means of estimating the calorie level consumed. However, the problem with this approach is the difficulty of getting reliable income or expenditure data in the subsistence agricultural economy where people get part or all of their food from own production (Maxwell and Smith, 1992). A related problem of income based approach as argued in Burchi and De Muro

(2012) is that it requires making several assumptions to logically move, step-by-step, from income or expenditure to food security. That is, to move from income/expenditure to food though price per unit information; then from food to calorie through equivalence tables; and lastly, from calorie availability to food security insecurity depending on the threshold.

2.1.3.2 Basic Needs/food first/Approach

The basic needs approach emerged in 1970s as alternative to 'growth models' for dealing with poverty and inequality (Degefa, 2005). According to Burchi and De Muro (2012), this approach was proposed by the International Labour Organisation (ILO) as new model of development. For the proponents of the basic needs approach, development is a process aiming at the satisfaction of basic needs of all people.

Though, the list of basic needs outlined by various authors varies slightly, food has emerged as the dominant basic need under this approach. This can be evidenced from the argument of Magrabi *et al.* (1991: 65) cited in Burchi and De Muro (2012) that "food is a basic need probably the most basic need of all". The Maslow's Need Hierarchy Theory based assertion of Handy (1985 : 30) quoted in Maxwell & Smith (1992 : 28) as "Lower order needs are dominant until satisfied, whereupon the higher order needs come into operation ... if you are starving, your needs for esteem or status will be unimportant; only food matters" and the argument of Hopkins (1986:4) also quoted in Maxwell & Smith (1992 : 28) as "— Access to necessary nutrients is fundamental, not only to life per se, but also to stable and enduring social order" can also be regarded as arguments supplementing the primacy position that food holds relative to other human needs. Generally, the basic needs based discourse in development literature has heavily affected the debate on food security by giving birth to what is called *food first* view (Burchi and De Muro 2012).

This approach considers food as a dominant basic need and priority element of food security. The framework focuses directly on whether people eat enough food and with this it contributed for further shifting of the analysis of food security from national/macro level to micro-level. The food security analysis methods such as food frequency assessment, direct observation of food consumption, and dietary diversity score fall under this framework and both individuals and households can be used as unit of analysis in the approach (Burchi and De Muro, 2012).

Comparing this view with the income based approach discussed above, Burchi and De Muro (2012) contends that the food first approach focuses on the commodity we are interested in, the food, rather than the income needed to buy a food and this, focusing directly on what is actually eaten, in turn avoids the problem arising from underestimation of the food grown at home.

However, this approach draws attention to short-term food security: it tells us whether households have enough food to feed all its members in a given time, or, eventually, in the past mas has been argued in (Burchi and De Muro, 2012).

2.1.3.4 Entitlement Approach

According to Degefa (2001), the origin of this approach, which is also considered as Food Entitlement Decline (FED) in (Maxwell and Smith, 1992), is traced back to the work of Sen (1981). It emerged as an alternative to FAD and argues that food availability in the economy orient the market does not necessarily entitle a person to consume, and famine can occur without decline in aggregate food availability (Degefa, 2005). Sen (1981:45) describes this approach as "The entitlement approach concentrates on each person's entitlements to commodity bundles including food, and views starvation as resulting from a failure to be entitled to a bundle with enough food." In the context of this theory, food insecurity can be conceptualised as the result of entitlement failure. In a way of affirming this view Sen (1981:7) says "— starvation — is a function of entitlements and not of food availability as such." An entitlement failure such as an inability to grow subsistence food (direct entitlements), an inability to exchange labour or property on the market (indirect entitlements), or an absence of adequate systems of public relief and social security (transfer entitlements) (Osmani 1999 in Tincani, 2012, Flaherty, 2013) may result in food insecurity.

According to Burchi and De Muro (2012), the groups that mostly face direct entitlement failure are food-producers and those who are exposed to trade /or indirect/entitlement failures are producers of commodities other than food: when their terms of exchange fall or when the total availability of food declines.

Though it was primarily meant for the analysis of famine (Burchi and De Muro, 2012), the entitlement approach has significantly affected the notion of food security and contributed for food security analysis by adding the access dimension. With this comes the belief that having enough food per capita at national level can only be a necessary condition but not sufficient condition for food security. Hence, making a food security assessment needs widening the informational basis by incorporating variables related to people's endowments such as productive and non-productive assets, intangible resources such as education and social capital as well as information on wage, and other prices of food and non-food items (Burchi and De Muro, 2012). With this framework, food security assessment can be conducted at micro level and both individuals and households can be the unit of analysis. This approach is also appreciated for its capacity to provide information on the future vulnerability to food insecurity as it considers full set of assets or resources.

2.1.3.5 Sustainable Livelihoods Approach

Sustainable Livelihood Framework (SLF) is general approach to the analysis of development issues such as poverty and food security. According to Burchi and De Muro (2012), the emphasis on livelihood started in the 1980s by Chambers (1983) who introduced the basic elements of this approach, with a focus on rural development and poverty. Ellis (2000:10) cited in Devereux (2004) conceptualises livelihoods as "the assets (natural, physical, human, financial and social capital), the activities, and the access to these (mediated by institutions and social relations) that together determine the living gained by individual or household." Chambers (1988) cited in Maxwell and Smith (1992) defined livelihood as adequate stocks and flows of food and cash to meet basic needs and linked sustainability with the maintenance or enhancement of resource productivity on the long term basis. A more comprehensive definition of sustainable livelihood is found in Chambers and Conway, (1991, p.6) in LIFT and USAID (2011:8) and Chambers and Conway (1992) in WFP (2009: 24) which says:

"A Livelihood comprises the capabilities, assets (stores, resources, claims, and access) and activities required for a means of living: a livelihood is sustainable which can cope with and recover from stress and shocks, maintain or enhance its capabilities and assets, and provide sustainable livelihood opportunities for the next generation; and which contributes net benefits to other livelihoods at the local and global levels in the short and long term."

The sustainable livelihood framework is more comprehensive approach as it includes the maintains of other approaches such as basic needs and entitlement approaches. It focuses both on gaining the living or necessities of life like basic needs approach and on means of securing living as the case in entitlement approach (Burchi and De Muro, 2012). At the core of SLF is as sets commanded by a household, which are very similar to the concept of "endowments" in the entitlement approach. The assets are classified into five categories: natural capital, physical capital, human capital, financial capital, social capital (Ellis, 2000 in Juma, 2009, LIFT and USAID 2011, Burchi and De Muro, 2012, Maxwell and Smith, 1992). The SLF also explicitly gives attention to the broader context such as political, economic, physical, social, and cultural and is also known for its long term perspectives. These features of it together with the consideration of household assets mentioned here has brought about three interrelated concepts to the analysis of food security: the concept of vulnerability, the idea of sustainability, and coping strategies that represent a set of activities that are undertaken by a household in response to shocks affecting food availability. The framework enables assessment of food security at micro level and household and community is the commonly used unit of analysis (Burchi and DeMuro, 2012).

2.1.3.6 Disaster Based Theory of Food Security

Disaster based theory was developed by Blaikie *et al.* (1994) cited in Degefa (2005) and Yasir (2009) and it was mainly meant for the analysis of vulnerability. The theory treats food insecurity as a disaster and argues that natural hazards cannot cause a disaster of food shortage unless combined with other human factors (Degefa, 2005). It argues that for disaster to happen there must be vulnerable people whose livelihood cannot withstand certain kinds of hazards (Degefa, 2005). According to Yasir (2009), disaster theory centre on the organised complexity of the interactions between natural hazards and human / institutional actions.

There exist two variants of disaster theories: pressure and Release (PAR) Model and Access Model. As cited in Degefa (2005: 79), Blaikie *et al.* (1994 : 22) explained the notion of PAR as "The basis for the PAR idea is that a disaster is the intersection of two opposing forces: those processes generating vulnerability on one side, and physical exposure to a hazard on the other. The 'release' idea is incorporated to conceptualise the reduction of disaster." According to Yasir (2009), PAR Model emphasises on the identification of various forces and their interactions at the macro level and the need to trace out the progression of vulnerability from the root causes to resultant unsafe conditions and their interaction with natural hazards. In the context of PAR, disaster, food insecurity in the context, is the outcome of the interaction between hazards and vulnerability, which in turn is produced by interaction between three factors: 'root causes' of a disaster, 'dynamic pressure', and the resultant 'unsafe conditions' in a way that dynamic pressures channeling root causes into unsafe conditions (Degefa, 2005).

According to Degefa (2005), the root causes that give rise to vulnerability, are economic, demographic, and political processes having hands on the allocation and distribution of resources between different groups of people. They can affect the level of rural household's vulnerability to food shortage either by providing or denying equal access to resources such land, for instance. The focus of Access model is on explaining how the unsafe conditions arise in relation to the economic and political processes that allocate assets, income, and other resources in a society (Degefa, 2005, Twigg, 2001). The main argument is that, individual's or household's relative access to resources is a function of class structure in a society and hence ones position within the society or community can determine its access to resources which in turn determine its level of vulnerability to hazard impact.

2.1.3.7 Human Development and Capability Approach

This is an approach proposed by (Burchi and De Muro 2012) based on, as they claim, insights from '*Hunger and Public Action*' book of Dreze and Sen (1989). The writers provide the following as the major innovations of the capability approach to food security (P: 18) : By switching the focus from "command over food" to "nutritional capabilities," this approach goes beyond the "access" dimension of food security – that is the main concern of the basic needs, entitlement and sustainable livelihood approaches– and includes also the "utilisation" dimension.

They further argue that, by analysing the phenomenon through the three steps, the capability approach situates the food security study within the broader topic of wellbeing. In explaining what makes this approach distinct from the other existing frameworks, the writers further say (P:27) :

The analysis of food security through the capability approach allows a more comprehensive examination of the phenomenon. While the income-based approach would take income as focal variable, the entitlement/capability approach provides information on how income is used to ultimately reach the capability to be food secure depending on personal and external conversion factors, food choices and behaviours.

Unlike the food-first approach, the capability approach takes into account the quality, utilisation and social acceptability of food, and the interaction with other basic capabilities such as health and education.

As a path to food security analysis under this framework, they proposed a three step procedure (1) analysis of '*food entitlements*', (2) analysis of '*basic capabilities*' for food security, and (3) analysis of the '*capability to be food secure*'. They argue that each phase implies adding a new informational basis, new variables, and new dimensions for the food security analysis.

2.3 Measuring Household's Food Security / Food Security Indicators

Abduselam (2017) says food security is a complex notion that is virtually impossible to measure directly. Barrett (2010) in Maxwell *et al.* (2013) argues for focusing food security measurement on the four major "pillars" of food security—availability, access, utilisation, and risk, which is also alternatively labeled as stability or vulnerability. Similarly, Coates and Maxwell (2012) cited in Maxwell *et al.* (2013) notes that the most desirable measures of food security, if available, would be a single measure that is valid and reliable, comparable over time and space, and which captures different elements of food security. However, despite the efforts made in looking for such a measure for decades, no single measure emerged as comprehensive enough to meet these criteria (Maxwell *et al.,* 2013 and Upton *et al.,* 2015).

One thing that can be learned from discussions in the above paragraphs, even if comprehensive review of indicators have not been made here, is that there is no single comprehensive measure of food security to rely on when it comes to food security assessment in general and at household level in particular. This is mainly because of the multidimensional nature of food security concept as Maxwell *et al.* (2013:12) meticulously put it: "The World Food Summit definition of food security, adopted and widely promoted by FAO, contains several key elements, or dimensions, each of them difficult enough to measure separately, but nearly impossible to measure in totality using any single indicator." Hence, the measurement of food security can obviously be more of a compromised one rather than absolutely perfect. Such a compromise can usually be a particular framework or theory moderated. However, in the situation where the theories themselves do focus only on one or the other aspect of the concept under consideration, as is true in the case of food security, the choice will be between fixating to a particular framework and measuring the aspect of a concept emphasised by it or trying to take a combined view of theories and finding indicators that cover their tents to the extent possible. When the choice is the later one, as is the case in the current study, the central meaning of the concept to be measured or under consideration, in effect takes the lead in guiding the measurement indicatorsselection. In the case of the current study, however, this doesn't preclude the role of the theories as the food security theories themselves focus on one or more dimensions of food security concept.

Coates (2013) cited in Maxwell *et al.* (2013) has provided a disaggregated descriptions to the major elements/dimensions of the food security definition which says "Food security exists when all people, at all times, have physical and economic access to sufficient, safe and nutritious food that meets their dietary needs and food preferences for an active and healthy life" (FAO, 2000; World Food Summit, 1996 in Maxwell *et al.,* 2013). According to Coates (2013) cited in Maxwell *et al.* (2013:12), the components embedded in the definition are: Quantity or Sufficiency (implied in the phrase … physical and economic access to sufficient…); Quality or Diversity (represented by a phrase…nutritious food that meets dietary needs…); Acceptability (embedded in the word …preferences…); Safety (linked to terms …safe…food); and Stability (implied in the phrase …at all times…). Cognizant of these components of food security that a given measure is ought to capture, Maxwell *et al.* (2013) have examined about seven indicators in terms of the dimensions of food security that each captures using an empirical work on northern Ethiopia. The indicators include coping strategy index (CSI), reduced coping strategy index (rCSI), household food insecurity access scale (HFIAS), household hunger score (HHS), food consumption score (FCS), household dietary diversity score (HDDS), and self-assessed food security (SAFS). They are argued for being rapid, accurate, and cross-contextual indicators of food security and for being mostly correlated individually with calorie based indicators in terms of identifying food security status (Maxwell *et al.*, 2013).

2.4 Food Security in Ethiopia

Ethiopia is the second most populous country in Africa with an estimated population of 94.3 million people in 2013 CSA (2013). As indicated by Africa Food Security and Hunger/ Undernourishment Multiple Indicator Scorecard, Ethiopia ranked as first in having the highest number of people in state of undernourishment/ hunger which is 32.1 million people. This makes it, the fourth African country scoring (37.1 percent) of the population being undernourished / in hunger African Development Bank (2014). The livelihoods of rural Ethiopian people are highly sensitive to climate. Food insecurity patterns are seasonal and linked to rainfall patterns, with hunger trends declining significantly after the rainy seasons. Climate related shocks affect productivity, hamper economic progress and exacerbate existing social and economic problems Anderson *et al.,* (2015). Food insecurity situation in Ethiopia is highly linked up to severe, recurring food shortage and famine, which are associated to recurrent drought. Currently there is a growing consensus that food insecurity and poverty problems are closely related in the Ethiopian context. Droughts and other related disasters (such as crop failure, water shortage, and livestock disease, land degradation, limited household assets, low income) are significant triggers, more important factors which increase vulnerability to food security and undermined livelihood MoARD (2009).

Ethiopia has been a net importer of food for more than three decades. In the decade between 1985 and 1994, net domestic production of cereals that on average account for about 85 percent of household food consumption ranged between 82.7 and 93.8 percent of total supply. Even though, different factors are contributing to vulnerability of the country which includes rapid population growth with low per capita income, rain-fed agriculture, under-development of water resources, land degradation, low economic development, and weak institutions. Drought, human and livestock diseases as well as resource-based conflicts are aggravating factors for the food insecurity situation in Ethiopia Fisseha, K., (2014).

About 10 percent of Ethiopia's citizens are chronically food insecure and this figure rises to more than 15 percent during the frequent drought years. World Food Programme found long-term effects of chronic malnutrition cost Ethiopia approximately 16.5 percent of its GDP each year. 2.7 million people will require emergency food assistance in 2014 and 238,761 children require treatment for severe acute malnutrition in 2014. Estimated number of food insecure people was 4.5 million August, 2015 and by the end of the same year this figure had more than doubled to 10.2 million Ethiopians UNICEF (2014).

2.5 Review of Some Empirical Studies

This section presents the summary of previously done similar works that have been accessed both directly and through others. The recent study conducted in Nicaragua by Cianiand Romano (2013) aims at developing a methodology for quantitative assessment of resilience to food insecurity and testing whether the pre-shock resilience score of households predict their post-shock food security status. Their study treated resilience as latent variable represented by a composite index comprising ten components. They have also attempted to show how a resilience index can be used as an instrument to policy evaluation. Following the line of Alinovi *et al.* (2008 and 2010), first each of the components is estimated separately and then combined to develop a resilience index. They observed positive relationship between pre-shock resilience index and post-shock food security status at household level. Their findings also reveal small and owners and agricultural wage workers as livelihood groups with poor resilience scores in the livelihood based disaggregation.

Alinovi *et al.* (2010) undertook a study in Kenya on household's resilience to food insecurity by applying the FOA's conceptual model that was developed in 2008 and first applied for the resilience study in Palestinian state. Both Alinovi *et al.* (2008 and 2010), treat resilience as a latent variable to be measured by composite index. In Alinovi *et al.* (2008), all the components in the FAO's framework have been used except assets, due to lack of data on it, in the composite resilience estimation. However, in Alinovi *et al.* (2010), the components or indicators of resilience have been modified to give contextual flavour considering the importance of farming in Kenya's population. The objective of the study was to measure empirically the outcomes of different livelihoods strategies in terms of household resilience to food insecurity in the specific context of Kenyan households. They found out that the large-holder farmers' livelihood cluster is the most resilient one while the pastoralist group being the least resilient. They also learned that the determinants of resilience found to be different for each livelihood group. Measurementwise, the authors have designed a two stage process to resilience assessment. In the first stage, the observed variables are used to estimate the first set of latent variables and the resulting latent variables are, in turn, used to estimate resilience index using the latent variable model (factor analysis).

Keil *et al.* (2008) as reported in Ciani and Romano (2013) use observable variables as a proxy of resilience rather than using the composite index. In their study, resilience is measured as the observed degree of drought induced expenditure reductions for basic necessities. The logic here seems that households whose basic necessity expenditure has fallen because of this shock are deemed to be non-resilient. In their treatment about who is resilient and non-resilient, they assumed that the absolute value of negative variations in the consumption expenditure is negatively correlated with resilience and fully resilient household is expected to show null variations of basic consumption. Here, one needs to note that, though related, as food is one of the basic consumption good, in this study, resilience is not directly indexed to food security rather it is attached to basic necessities in general.

2.6 Impact of Disasters on Food Security

Disasters pose direct and indirect threats to the livelihoods and food security of smallholder farmers. The number of people in need of food assistance often increases after the occurrence of disasters, especially when vulnerable populations are affected. The 2015–2016 El Niño-related droughts and floods, for instance, heavily affected the food security and nutritional status of more than 60 million people globally (FAO, 2016). The uncertainty associated with the observed increase in the frequency and intensity of disasters in many developing countries can drive poor farmers to invest in low-risk but low-returning agricultural production technologies and techniques (Cole *et al.*, 2013). In turn, low investments can lead to lower future farm profits and increased food insecurity (Aimin, 2010).

Furthermore, the impact of disasters on reduced food consumption, education and healthcare can lead to long-term negative effects in terms of income generation and future food security (FAO, 2015c).

Food insecurity and disaster risk reinforce one another. Disasters have shattering consequences on food security, and food-insecurity increases vulnerability, leading to a downward spiral in which rural livelihoods are increasingly eroded (Garschagen *et al.*, 2015). In disaster situations, food-insecure people might find themselves forced to take desperate measures to address immediate needs, often compromising their livelihoods and increasing their vulnerability and exposure.

2.7. Severe Droughts

Drought can force food-insecure farmers to over exploit common property resources such as community forests, pasture, ponds, riverbanks and groundwater, with negative medium- and long-term consequences for agricultural productivity and food security (Pandey *et al.*, 2007).

2.8. Conceptual Framework

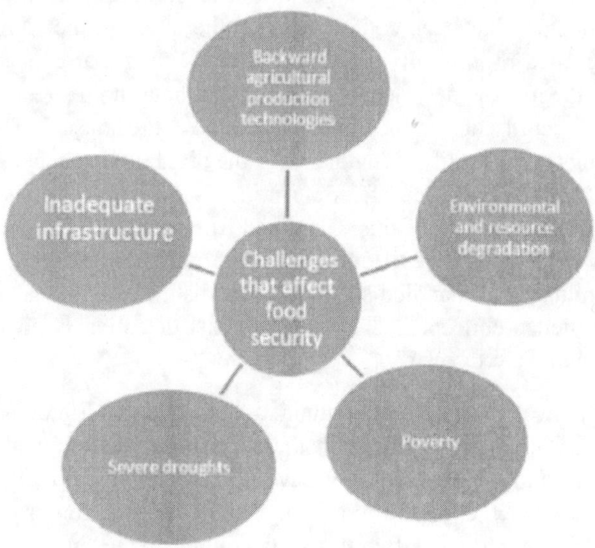

Source: Own survey@ 2020.

2.9 Local Studies

Mulat and Negussie (2013) undertook a study to identify determinants of sustainable resilience for food and nutrition security of farming rural households, using Ethiopian Rural Households' Survey (ERHS) data of 1994 to 2004. They estimated household's resilience to food insecurity as latent variable composed of four components: grain held in stock, in-kind precautionary savings, investment in child education, and participation in mutual aid association (Idir). They employed principal component analysis for measuring resilience and dynamic probit random effect model to find determinants of dynamics of household's resilience. Their study shows a true state (path) - dependence on dynamics of household resilience to food insecurity and positive and significant correlation between sustainable resilience to food insecurity and the following factors: land under cultivation; ownership of oxen, milking cows and transport animals, use of improved technologies, and membership in traditional saving groups (Iqub).

However, the survey used by the researchers is limited in terms of coverage. Only few villages are covered and areas where the current study has been conducted and other areas in the vicinity are not reached by this survey. Also it is my feeling that conceptually, given the most widely accepted notion that household's resilience to food insecurity lies on the options available to the household to make a living and its ability to handle risks, the dividing line between what they call it resilience and determinants of its dynamics is not indisputable. In line of this, Ciani and Romano (2013) argue that in the works where resilience measurement and search for its determinants are handled separately, the distinction of measurement of resilience concept and its determinants detection is not always clear and easy to justify.

Maxwell *et al.* (2013), in their study in northern Ethiopia, in two woredas of Tigray region, considered resilience as one component of their study. However, they have not measured it directly. Their study traced the livelihood change over time in four rounds of household survey over two years: two rounds in the "hunger" season and two rounds in the "postharvest" season.

In more specific terms, their study tracks household's food security status in each round, looks for its determinants, and changes in livelihoods, in particular the dynamics of asset accumulation or loss. The findings of the study have shown steady improvements in households' food security indicators without a corresponding improvement in the level of assets at the household level, with poverty traps being suspected source to blame.

Mulugeta (2014) undertook a study on resilience to drought induced food insecurity shocks in two districts of Borana Zone of Oromia Region. He conceptualised resilience as a recovery or ability of people to rehabilitate their livelihood assets to pre-drought level and relied on household's own assessment about the extent of recovery as a way of measuring resilience. The study considered lack of adequate social services as a potential barrier to improved resilience. Herd mobility, literacy, sanitation, and social networks have been identified as factors strongly linked with shock absorption capacity. More recently, Guyu and Muluneh (2015) undertook a study on household's resilience to seasonal food insecurity in north-western Ethiopia. They estimated household's resilience in two stages treating resilience as a latent variable. Their findings reveal that the resilience capacity of households in the study area is very weak and households in the indigenous ethno-culture group are much less resilient than the non-indigenous ones. Therefore, this study will assess Food Security Programme during Disaster and its Problems and Challenges in the case of Afar Region, Dewe district, Ethiopia.

3

Research Methodology

3.1 Study Area

Deweis one of the woredas in the Afar Region of Ethiopia. Part of the Administrative Zone 5, Dewe is located near the base of the eastern escarpment of the Ethiopian highlands, and bordered on the south by the Borkana River which separates it from Dalifage and HadeleEle, on the west by the Amhara Region, on the north by Telalak, and on the east by Administrative Zone 3. The major settlement in this woreda is Wedarage. Dewe was the seat of the Sultanate of Dewe, one of the Afar's traditional sultanates in the Afar Region.

The average elevation in this woreda is 802 meters above sea level Hailu. Ejara (2011). Rivers in this woreda include the Awash, which divides it into eastern and western parts. As of 2008, Dewe has 58 kilometers of community roads; about 29 percent of the total population has access to drinking water and 95 percent Health access. This means; 3 Health Centers and 12 Health Posts functionals in the woreda Census (2007).

Based on the 2007 Census conducted by the Central Statistical Agency of Ethiopia (CSA), this woreda has a total population of 42,397, of whom 24,865 are men and 17,532 women; with an area of 760.90 square kilometers, Dewe has a population density of 55.72. While 2,280 or 5.38 percent are urban inhabitants, a further 12,994 or 30.65 percent are pastoralists. A total of 5,376 households were counted in this woreda, which results in an average of 7.9 persons to a household, and 6,200 housing units. 99.55 percent of the population said they were Muslim Census (2007).

3.2 Research Design

According to Saunders *et al.* (2007), research design is the general plan of how a researcher will go about answering the research question (s). For a particular research, design decisions are commonly made with respect to research strategies, research choices and time horizons (Robson, 2002 in Saunders *et al.* 2007). Regarding time horizon, the current study is cross-sectional one. That is, the data was gathered from different cross-sections, households in this case, at one point in time only. The study employed survey as its research strategy and dominantly used quantitative approach with qualitative triangulation when it comes to research choice. That is, it adapted mixed method research design (sequentially explanatory) as a research approach. The specific methods related to research design of the current study have been discussed in the upcoming sub-sections.

3.3 Sampling Techniques

The study was adopted a stratified random sampling method in the sampling of the population. The study was selected by using stratified simple random sampling. As a result the population under study is categorised into specific strata's. It is common practice in research work to use sample in order to generalise about the targeted populations. The size of sample and the technique used to draw sample from the population; however, depends on the availability of time, money, personnel and information. A different sampling paradigm by Lowler (1984) noted that there is not a single precise way for the determinations of sample size hence there are a number of inadequacy for deciding on sample size.

3.3.1 Sample Size

Based on the 2007 Census conducted by the Central Statistical Agency of Ethiopia (CSA), this woreda has a total population of 42,397. As a result, in quantitative research, the sample size was determined using a statistical formula. Since the quantitative research sample size is determined using a statistical formula, quantitative research is intentionally random sampling. For this study, to determine sample size, the researcher used Kothari (2004) formula set for the case of a finite population. To make it easier to manage sample size and to control systematic error, the researcher has taken a 95 percent level of confidence and an estimation error of +5 percentlevel of precision. Even though the sample size determination has been exhibited by the table, the researcher needed to calculate the necessary sample size by combining the desired precision and confidence of level to increase its reliability and validity. For the quantitative study, different authors use different formulas to determine the sample size. Accordingly, the sample size of the respondents has been calculated by using the following formula.

Therefore,

$$n = \frac{Z^2 \ p.q.N}{e^2 \ (N-1) + Z^2.p.q}$$

Where, n is the desired sample size, N is total population of households, in three kebeles, Z is 1.96 that is t-value for 95 percent of confidence level, p is an estimation of variance (0.5 percent),q is (1-p) which is equal to 0.5, and e is an estimation error of sampling which is = 5 percent = 0.05

Hence,

$$n = \frac{(1.96)^2 (0.5)(0.5)42397407.1807}{(.05)^2 \ (2288-1) + (1.96)^2 (0.5)(0.5)} = \frac{61}{6.6779}$$

Therefore, 61 households were the sample size of the study.

3.4 Methods of Data Collection

Research methods are specific techniques/methods of data collection and analysis are used to achieve the broad research objective through addressing the specific objectives of the study. To address the research problem the researcher used semi-structured and structured questionnaire. The reason to implement self-administered closed-ended and open-ended questionnaire is because of its importance to reveal detail information for the study.

In-depth interview is an effective qualitative method for getting people to talk about their personal feelings, opinions, and experiences.

3.4.1 Questionnaire

According to Walonick (1993), the Questionnaire is one of the most popular methods of collecting data conduction in scholarly research. It provides convenient way of gathering information from a total target population. As a result, questionnaire was used to gather information through quantitative and qualitative data.

3.4.2 Interview

Interview is carried out as instrument of data collection to gather data on the topic of the study. Creswell (2009) suggested that interview would be used to elicit views and opinions from the participants in detail. Interview is carried out as instrument of data collection to gather data on the topic of the study. Creswell (2009) Suggested that interview would be used to elicit views and opinions from the participants in detail. Therefore, five officials were selected purposively for an interview.

3.5 Data Analysis Methods

Kerlinger (1986) defines data analysis as categorising, manipulating and summarising of data in order to obtain answers to research questions. As it is stated under the sub-topic of 'research methodology', this research is of descriptive type. Accordingly, for realisation and successful accomplishment of the study, data collected from different primary and secondary sources was recorded, edited. For data analysis SPSS software was used. The qualitative data was analysed using thematic analysis.

3.6 Ethical Considerations

During the whole process of the study, the researcher would try to obey and strictly follow ethical issues. The researcher understands that ethical consideration is very critical to protect the respondents and to feel protected at all times. The researcher is reach to consent by explaining the significance of the study and inform the subjects that their responses would be used only for the purpose of the study. When the respondents agree to be involved in the study, steps is taken to ensure that they know exactly what they are agreeing to. The researcher ensured that the confidentiality and anonymity of the participants is maintained through the removal of any identified characteristics before widespread dissemination of information. The questionnaire was accompanied by opening letter which explained the purpose and significance of the study. The researcher makes clear that the participants name is not be used for any other purpose than this study.

4

Data Analysis and Interpretation

4.1 Introduction

The main intention of this chapter is presenting findings/results and discussing the data obtained during data gathering process for the problem under study. The results and discussions going to be presented in this case were to assess Food Security Programme during Disaster and its Problems and Challenges in the case of Afar Region, Dewe district, Ethiopia.The research questions intended to be answered are analysed as follows:-

Accordingly, 61 households were the sample size of the study. Therefore, the findings and results are presented as follow.

4.2 Response Rate

To get relevant information from different target groups 61 questionnaires were distributed for respondents. All 61 of the questionnaires distributed were collected as per the guidelines prepared. Therefore, the response rate was 100 percent.

4.3 Respondents Profiles

The first table showed the general background of the respondent's sex and age.

4.4 General Information of the Respondents

4.4.1 Respondents Biographical Background: Sex and Age of Respondents

Table 4.1: Sex of Respondents

Items	Sex					
	M	%	F	%	Total	%
	40	65.57	21	34.43	61	100

Source: own survey 2020

According to Table 4.1 above, 40 (65.57 percent) are males while 21 (34.43 percent) are females. This shows that most of the respondents were males followed by females respectively.

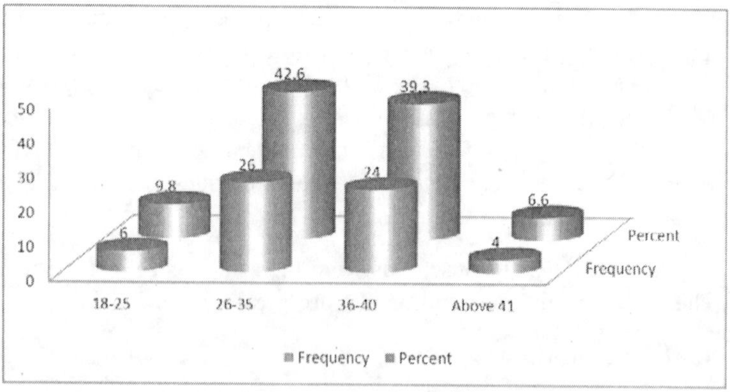

Fig. 4.1: Age of Respondents.

Source: Own Survey 2020

Regarding ages of the respondents, 26 (42.62 percent) of the respondents were between 26-35 years while 24 (39.34 percent) of the respondents were between 36-40 years while 6 (9.83 percent) of the respondents were 18 to 25 while 4 (6.55 percent) of the respondents were > 41 years old. This implies that majority of the respondents were between 26-35 years followed by 36-40 years.

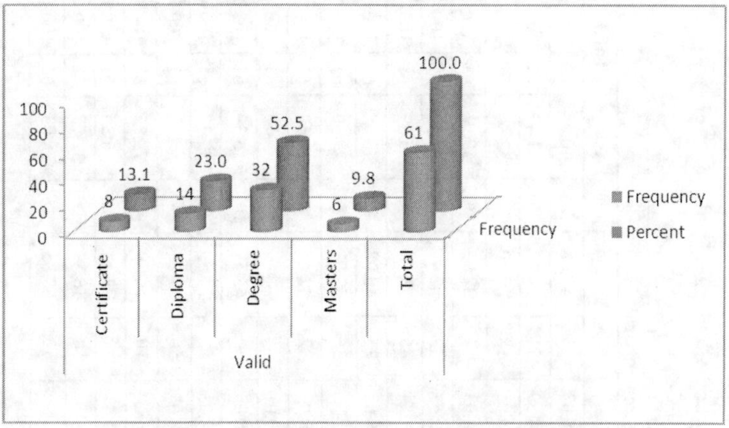

Fig. 4.2: Academic Qualification of Respondents.

Source: Own Survey 2020.

According to the Fig. 4.2, 32 (52.5 percent) of the respondents were degree holders, 14 (23 percent) of the respondents were diploma holders, 8 (13.1 percent) of the respondents were certificate holders while 6 (9.8 percent) of the respondents were Masters holders respectively. This implies that majority of the respondents were degree and diploma holders respectively. Respondents' educational backgrounds also have showed that there is an opportunity for leadership development since leadership position requires educational exposure.

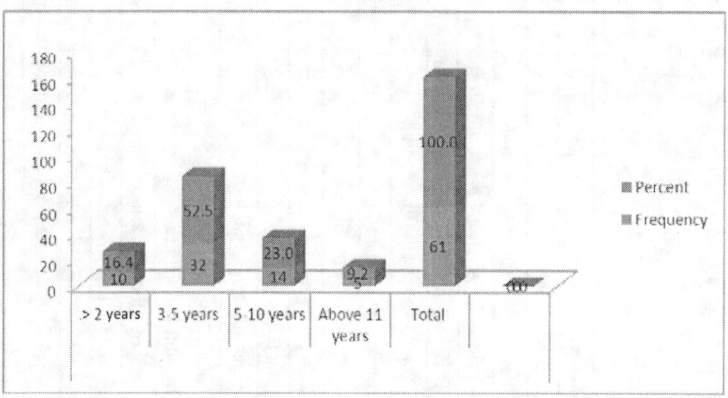

Fig. 4.3: Respondents Experience on their Current Position.

Source: Own Survey 2020

Table 4.2: Food Security Programme during Disaster and its Problems and Challenges in the case of Afar Region, Dewe district, Ethiopia

No.	Items	Agreement Scale											
		SDA		DA		NE		A		SA		Total	
1	Poverty	-	-	-	-	11	18.03	25	40.98	25	40.98	61	100
2	Severe droughts	11	18.03	7	11.47	15	24.59	21	34.42	7	11.47	61	100
3	Inadequate infrastructure	-	-	-	-	11	18.03	18	29.50	32	52.45	61	100
4	Backward agricultural production technologies	-	-	-	-	11	18.03	14	22.95	36	59.01	61	100
5	Environmental and resource degradation	-	-	7	11.47	4	6.557	32	52.45	18	29.50	61	100
6	Lack of adequate skills/training	-	-	-	-	6	9.83	45	73.77	10	16.39	61	100
7	Lack of technical support	-	-	-	-	11	18.03	25	40.98	25	40.98	61	100
8	Lack of basic facilities			11	18.03	-	-	36	59.01	14	29.50	61	100
9	Low salary and non-existence of incentives	-	-	-	-	11	18.03	32	52.45	18	29.50	61	100
10	Population pressure	11	81.03	14	29.50	36	59.01	-	-	-	-	61	100
11	Limitations in technology	-	-	-	-	11	18.03	40	65.57	10	16.39	61	100
12	Lack of access to inputs	-	-	-	-	11	18.03	15	24.59	35	57.37	61	100
13	Instability due to problems of adjustment	-	-	-	-	11	18.03	50	-	-	-	61	100
14	Lack of adequate skills/training	-	-	-	-	6	9.83	10	16.39	45	73.77	61	100
15	Limited access to basic services	-	-	-	-	7	11.47	44	72.13	10	16.39	61	100
16	Lack of product diversification and market integration	-	-	5	8.19	16	9.83	10	16.39	20	32.78	61	100
17	Limited capacity in planning and implementation	-	-	8	13.11	-	-	42	68.85	11	18.03	61	100

Source: Own survey 2020.

As it can be seen from the figure above, 32 (52.5 percent) of the respondents were 3-5 years of an experience on the current position, 14 (23 percent) of the respondents have an experience of 5-10 years on the current position, 10 (16.4 percent) of the respondents have an experience of >2 years on the current position while 5 (9.2 percent) of the respondents have an experience of above 11 years respectively.

In relation to their experience, the majority of the respondents have advantage of life experience to contribute to leadership development.

According to the Table 4.2, for the question 'Poverty' 25 (40.98 percent) of the respondents said A and SA while 11 (18.03 percent) of the respondents said NE respectively. This means that there is poverty and it is a big challenge.

The data obtained from an interview supported this view in that:

The food price crisis reveals the need to give greater attention to the political dimensions of food security when providing economic policy advice to Ethiopian governments. The challenge for policy-makers is to find a reasonably efficient and politically acceptable balance between supply and price management, subsidies, safety nets, and other Programmes to protect the poor without simultaneously suppressing the price incentives to farmers that encourage their supply response.

Likely, for 'Severe droughts' 21 (34.42 percent) of the respondents said A, 15 (24.59 percent) of the respondents said NE, 11 (18.03 percent) of the respondents said SDA, 7 (11.47 percent) of the respondents said DA and SA respectively. This implies that severe drought is a big challenge.

The complexity of the issues arising from the food price crisis argues for much stronger coordination with other international and regional organisations. No single institution has all the skills and resources necessary to address the challenges of food security.

In similar vein, for 'Inadequate infrastructure' 32 (52.45 percent) of the respondents said SA, 18 (29.50 percent) of the respondents said A while 11 (18.03 percent) of the respondents said NE. This indicates that an inadequate infrastructure is serious challenge. For the question 'backward agricultural production technologies' 36 (59.01 percent) of the respondents said SA, 14 (22.95 percent) of the respondents said A while 11 (18.03 percent) of the respondents said NE. This means that a backward agricultural production technology has a big challenge on food security.

The data obtained from an interview supported this idea that:

Looking forward, the review of the recent food price crisis and an understanding of the transformation process from an agrarian to urban society highlights long-run challenges for sustaining Dewe district food security and promoting inclusive rural growth.

First, there is an urgent need to revitalise growth in agricultural productivity and simultaneously to address the increasingly tangible impacts of climate change on agriculture. Climate change is often thought of as a longer-run threat, but there is accumulating empirical evidence that rising average temperatures, extreme heat events, rising atmospheric ozone levels, and other climate related phenomena are already adversely affecting agricultural productivity. To some degree, it will be possible to adapt to climate change through the application of existing technologies for conservation agriculture. More efficient use of irrigation water will also be critical, particularly in Afar region. During the coming decades, the scientific challenges of adapting agriculture to climate change will be formidable. Evaluation shows that investment in agricultural research has an enormous economic payoff, but it is a long-run process requiring sustained commitment from international and national research centers as well as the private sector.

As it can be seen from the table above for question 'Environmental and resource degradation' 32 (52.45 percent) of the respondents said A, 18 (29.50 percent) of the respondents said SA, 7 (11.47 percent) of the respondents said DA while 4 (57 percent) of the respondents said NE. This implies that there is environmental and resource degradation. The data obtained from an interview supported in that;

Households with heads without education recorded the highest incidence of food insecurity. More importantly however, is that, fewer people are expected to be vulnerable relative to the observed (actual) food insecurity for households with secondary and/or above education. There is an evidence of higher level of food insecurity among rural farming households (whether predicted or observed) when compared to their rural non-farming households' counterpart.

For the question 'Lack of adequate skills/training' 45 (73.77 percent) of the respondents said A, 10 (16.39 percent) of the respondents said SA while 6 (9.83 percent) of the respondents said NE. This implies that there is lack of adequate skills/training in the organisation.

For the question 'Lack of technical support' 25 (40.98 percent) of the respondents said SA and A while 11 (18.03 percent) of the respondents said NE. This shows that there is lack of technical support in the organisation. For the question 'Lack of basic facilities' 36 (59.01 percent) of the respondents said A, 14 (29.50 percent) of the respondents said SA while 11 (18.03 percent) of the respondents said DA. This said that there is lack of basic facilities in the organisation.

The data obtained from an interview supported this idea in that:

The complexity of the issues arising from the food price crisis argues for much stronger coordination with other international and regional organisations. No single institution has all the skills and resources necessary to address the challenges of food security.

For the question 'Low salary and non-existence of incentives' 32 (52.45 percent) of the respondents said A, 18 (29.50 percent) of the respondents said SA while 11 (18.03 percent) of the respondents said NE. This implies that there is low salary and non-existence of incentives in the organisation. According to the Table 4.2, for the question 'Population pressure' 36 (59.01 percent) of the respondents said NE, 14 (29.50 percent) of the respondents said DA while 11 (18.03 percent) of the respondents said SDA. This indicates that there is population pressure in the organisation. For the question' Limitations in technology'40 (65.57 percent) of the respondents said A, 11 (18.03 percent) of the respondents said NE while 10 (16.39 percent) of the respondents said SA. This means that there is limitations in technology. For the question 'Lack of access to inputs'

35 (57.37 percent) of the respondents said SA, 15 (24.59 percent) of the respondents said A while 11 (18.03 percent) of the respondents said NE.

The data obtained from an interview supported in that;

In a disaster response, the lack of land tenure and documentation of individuals living in slums as well as an absence of active local government increasing the need to be proactive, rather than reactive. There are different disasters affect food security the main barriers include a lack of financial resources, poor access to information on climate adaptation, complex land tenure systems, and social-cultural factors. Furthermore, the lack of farm implements and machinery, lack of ready markets and limited access and high cost of improved varieties of crops are serious constraints to effective implementation of appropriate climate adaptation strategies by households.

This shows that there is lack of access to inputs in the organisation. For the 'instability due to problems of adjustment' 50 (81.96 percent) of the respondents said A, 11 (18.03 percent) of the respondents said NE. This shows that there instability due to problems of adjustment in the organisation.

As it can be seen from the Table 4.2 for the question 'Lack of adequate skills/training' 45 (73.77 percent) of the respondents said SA, 10 (16.39 percent) of the respondents said A while 6 (9.83 percent) of the respondents said NE. This indicates that there is lack of adequate skills/training in the organisation.

For the question 'Limited access to basic services' 44 (72.13 percent) of the respondents said A, 10 (16.39 percent) of the respondents said SA while 6 (9.83 percent) of the respondents said NE. This means that there is limited access to basic services in the organisation. Similarly, for the question 'Lack of product diversification and market integration' 20 (32.78 percent) of the respondents said SA, 16 (9.83 percent) of the respondents said NE while 5 (8.19 percent) of the respondents said DA. This implies that there is lack of product diversification and market integration in the organisation.

The data obtained from an interview supported in that:

The vulnerability estimates of households in the region indicate that there are a substantial proportion of households vulnerable to food insecurity. The results are highly heterogeneous across the zones, reflecting the differing socioeconomic conditions in each zone. Evidence from profiles also highlighted some of the characteristics distinctly related to vulnerability, such as residence in Afar region of Dewe district, larger family size relatively smaller farm size per adult equivalent and low education of the household head.

Lastly, for the question 'Limited capacity in planning and implementation' 42 (68.85 percent) of the respondents said A, 11 (18.03 percent) of the respondents said SA while 8 (13.11 percent) of the respondents said DA. This shows that there is limited capacity in planning and implementation in the organisation.

The data obtained from an interview supported this view in that:

The complexity of the issues arising from the food price crisis argues for much stronger coordination with other international and regional organisations. No single institution has all the skills and resources necessary to address the challenges of food security.

5

Summary, Conclusions and Recommendations

5.1 Introduction

The research investigated three interrelated empirical research questions. The first chapter has presented them together with the background and justification regarding relevance of undertaking the study. In the second chapter, the effort was geared towards providing theoretical and conceptual underpinnings and hence relevant literatures have been reviewed. In the third chapter, methodological issues have been discussed and appropriate methods of data analysis have been identified /specified for the investigated objectives. Using the identified methods of analysis for each research objectives, data analyses were done in the subsequent two chapters. So, the current chapter provides the summary of the findings of the analyses and conclusions drawn from them, policy recommendations, and contribution or theoretical implication of the current study.

5.2 Summary

This chapter focuses on the summary of the major findings of the study, conclusions and recommendations forwarded in the light of the major findings. The main objective of this study was, to assess Food Security Programme during Disaster and its Problems and Challenges in the case of Afar Region of Dewe district, Ethiopia. The study mainly used primary data through conducting purposive and random techniques.

This study sought answers to the following questions:-

- How disasters affect food security in the case of Afar Region of Dewe district, Ethiopia?
- What is the current rate of food insecurity in the research area?
- Who is vulnerable to food insecurity and what are the characteristics of households with vulnerability?
- Do the characteristics featuring households with food insecurity and households with vulnerability differ?
- What are the challenges influencing food security in the case of Afar Region of Dewe district, Ethiopia?

5.3 Conclusion

Based on the data obtained from results of the study, the following conclusions were made.

- Ethiopia is facing a massive drought and food insecurity crisis over the years. Drought, recurring food shortage and famine are great challenges faced by Ethiopian people. Different studies on current food security situation in the country show that there is a growing consensus that food insecurity, famine and poverty problems are closely related in the Ethiopian context in which drought and weather related shocks are the main driving forces.
- Regarding the current study, agricultural asset, income and food access, agricultural technology adoption, social capital, access to basic services, and adaptive capacity, as expected appear to have substantive importance for rural household's resilience to food insecurity. Hence, based on the very notion of resilience and the findings reported here, it can be concluded that the study areas households with higher possession of each of these resources can better cope with shocks and be able to maintain their food security in the face of shocks and stressors. Therefore, any efforts or interventions to be made to increase resilience of the study areas households need to focus on strengthening these capacity dimensions. However, the actors like local level government offices such as district level Agricultural Bureaus and NGOs need to reexamine the

role of social safety nets, specially the implementation aspect, in the study areas context. Specially, the focus of humanitarian aid that is made in response to draught and crop failure induced food insecurity should be made to have a role in guarding against productive assets erosion. So, the conclusion is that unless sound and well planned intervention is taken, most of the study area households can easily lose their food security status to worse even by a very meager shock.

- Though the majority of the surveyed households are not resilient in general, the inter livelihood systems or zones resilience analysis revealed that the household's level of resilience vary based on the livelihood systems.
- The implication is that resilience capacity building interventions require identifying the denominators to which the differences can be attributed. Specially, looking for a way of addressing population pressure on land and improving agricultural assets possessions of individual households can be good intervention priority for coffee and maize livelihood systems.
- Reducing the youths' demand for parents land share through designing and properly implementing alternative job packages can be a workable policy options for long term solution.
- Giving due emphasis to the agricultural intensification or technological factors such as supplying improved seeds and fertilisers with the goal of making them more workable and effective can be a commendable option for short term. Hence, giving attention to these areas need to be among the priorities of resilience capacity building interventions.
- The combination of factors has contributed to the food insecurity problem of the Afar Region, Dewe district, Ethiopia: irregular rain, land fragmentation, and population pressure.
- It has also been learned that the surveyed households employed a combination of various coping strategies, both consumption and non-consumption based, as a response to food insecurity problems.

- The analysis of the data on non-consumption based coping strategies utilised over the last two years period also revealed that the households responded to food insecurity shocks by utilising a range coping mechanisms. These findings has the implication that depending on the initial state of the households who utilised them, some of these coping mechanisms can lead them to the poverty trap and erode their ability to cope similar problems in the future. If not properly managed, even the coping strategy that doesn't have immediate individual impact, selling firewood in the current study's case, may not be environmentally sustainable.

5.5 Policy Implications

Based on observations both from the survey and key informants interview, the study makes the following recommendations.

- Resilience has become an important concept in the analysis of development issues such as household's food security. Resilient households can maintain their food security in the event of shocks or more quickly recovery from the effect of shocks as compared to then on-resilient counterparts. This warrants strengthening the resilience capacity of households if they can maintain their food security withstanding the effect of shocks.

- Strengthening resilience through intervention in turn requires understanding where their resilience capacity lies as it enables building on the existing strengths. Regarding Afara region Dewe District the current study found that income and food access, agricultural asset, and agricultural technology adaptation are the most contributing variables to over all resilience. Hence, finding out ways of improving food access, increasing agricultural asset possession, and ensuring access to and effective utilisation of agricultural technologies are among areas that can boost up rural household's resilience to food insecurity.

- The Agro-pastoralist Livelihood Dewe District based households are found to be weaker on average on access to basic services proxied through access to safe water, MFI, and telephone and adaptive capacity which is proxied through education, health, dependency ratio, and diversity of income sources dimensions of resilience. In some of these individual variables cases, this could be due to location that this zone is situated in relation to the center. Hence, planning for action by assessing the relative size of the problems in each of these areas can be good entry point for resilience capacity building interventions.

- Households can respond to shocks and resist its effects mainly based on the resources they possess. The external support made to them in the event of shocks can contribute best to resilience building if they are geared towards not only to life saving but also to that of saving household's productive assets and resources. This is how the resilience approach has bridged the gap between humanitarian emergency and development efforts by bringing them together. However, it doesn't seem this is the case in Dewe District as per the study's statistical finding, which is well supported by the key informants' interview. The policy implication is that, specially, the food related aid component of the social safety nets need to be redressed implementation-wise so as to make it support the livelihood assets saving efforts of the households in the event of food insecurity shocks.

- Food security situation of sizeable proportion of the survived households is not found satisfactory in almost all aspects of food security that the proxy measures employed in this survey can capture. For instance, very large proportion of the study households experienced worries of varying level with the indication that stable access and availability of food is a concern for the study area. The key informants' insight on the problem revealed that a multitude of factors are working to cause this problem though the extent of effect of each may not be equal for all livelihood zones.

- Encouraging and well supporting the livelihoods or income diversification efforts of the farmers is also a worthy policy option on Reducing the youth's demand for already highly fragmented land holdings by wisely designing and carefully implementing alternative job options.

5.6 Theoretical Implications

Using resilience approach to the analysis of development issues in general and food security analysis in particular is the recent one. As argued in literatures, regarding food security, it is the vulnerability analysis that has dominated most of the scholarly works for long. However, recently the concept of resilience has emerged as a new organising concept and resilience approach to food security analysis has been gaining wider acceptance. The current study is one of the few studies that have adapted such an approach, which is currently gaining momentum. In addition to adapting resilience approach, the current study has contributed to the existing literature in the following ways:

- Studies I come across with are either food security and coping strategy focused or resilience focused. Those that bring them together are rarely found. The exception in this case is Ciani and Romano (2013) who examined the relationship between food security and resilience as way to validate methodology they proposed for resilience to food insecurity analysis. Literatures have widely covered, at conceptual level, the possible impact of the nature of coping strategies employed by households on their resilience to food insecurity. However, to the best of my knowledge, none of the previous studies on household's resilience to food insecurity have empirically explored them. The current study has bridged this knowledge gap in the existing literature by empirically examining the linkage between the nature of previously employed coping strategies and household's resilience to food insecurity.

- Literatures argue for the value of combining resilience analysis with livelihood strategies pursued by households. This makes it possible to analyse different level of resilience to food insecurity achieved by various livelihood groups as well as the different strategies pursued by such groups in order to gain resilience to food insecurity. The current study too has also linked the analysis of household's resilience to food insecurity to livelihood systems, or livelihood choice as viewed from households stand point, by employing appropriate method of analysis.

- The existing works on quantitative analysis of household's resilience to food insecurity have not given sufficient emphasis to social capital. Though Guyu and Muluneh (2015) have captured it well with the variable they named as 'Cultural-bond-Reciprocity and Practices (CLRBP)', their focus was only on social capital proxies that were actually take place such as whether a household had been involved in hosting gust and/ or being hosted as a gust and fed. However, in such treatment, there is a room that a household who did not previously involved in such activity by chance but having a potential to do so if occasions leading to that happened would receive zero score and hence would be potentially treated as non-resilient. This indicates the need for incorporating some proxies of social capital that is not yet demonstrated in action. So, the current study has bridged this gap in the resilience literature by using perceived social capital, a latent variable in the case of current study, as one indicator of social capital.

- Though a couple of empirical works can be found on food security in the current study area, most of them have not brought in to picture differences in livelihood system/zones regarding food security situation. The study of Bechaye (2011) can be taken as exception in this regard. Bechaye (2011) has simply compared the average calorie intake of the three livelihood zones. However, as the study was based on sample, the observed mean difference might happen by chance and may not reflect the real difference among the livelihood groups. The application of more sound method, ANOVA in this case, for the analysis of food security situation among livelihood groups is methodological improvement of the current study in the context.

- The current study has also bridges the research gaps in terms of geographical coverage regarding household's resilience to food insecurity. In this regard, it has contributed context based evidence on household's resilience to food insecurity too.

5.7 Recommendations

In order to avoid, combating and preventing new food crises appear necessary to:

- Carry out a process of assessment and selection of the most effective best practices at an international, national and local level, in order to create food stocks and raw materials, defining the costs, timescales and roles of a similar process of global "assurance".
- At the same time, it is essential to define a new system of rules for the food commodities markets, capable of defending the role of the products exchanged in the markets not only from the economic perspective (e.g. envisaging forms of active surveillance by an independent authority or imposing "position limits" in order to guarantee that the sums invested do not involve operations of an excessively speculative nature).
- Governments commit to take comprehensive action to strengthen the longer-term productivity, sustainability, and resilience of the food and agriculture system worldwide, encompassing several elements.
- Improve food and agriculture innovation systems, encompassing public and private investments in scientific research and development, technology transfer, education, training, advisory services and ensure that successful practices are scaled up.
- Strengthen the CGIAR system to support technological innovation and global dissemination of technology, in particular to improve productivity performance in less developed countries taking into account the needs of smallholder and especially women farmers.
- Support the development of technologies and provide the appropriate incentives to address challenges specific to climate change and sustainable resource use (land and water).
- Increase public (official development assistance [ODA] and national governments) investment in developing country

agriculture, and in activities strongly linked to agricultural productivity growth, such as agricultural institutions, extension services, roads, ports, power, storage, irrigation systems and information and communication technology, where appropriate. Link public investment to the provision of sustainable public-private-civil society partnerships.

- Support comprehensive national food security strategies that are country-owned and led, evidence-based and inclusive of civil society and farmer organisations. In this respect, follow up such as the fund the Global Agriculture and Food Security Programme.

- Provide the enabling environment for farmers and other private sector actors to scale up investments, above and beyond ODA and national government spending, to achieve the increased productivity and enhanced resilience on which long term food security will depend.

- To elicit the needed level of private sector investment, less developed countries in particular will need to support introduction of effective governance systems and institutions, stable macroeconomic conditions, sound structural policies, human capital development and public services.

- Expediting Humanitarian Food Aid, especially World Food Programmeme.

- Develop an operational definition of a critical food shortage situation that might justify consideration of an export restricting measure. An export ban would be defined as a time limited measure of last resort, allowed only when other measures, including triggering domestic safety net measures for the poorest, have been exhausted, and taking into account, in particular, the food security needs of least developed countries and net food importing developing countries.

- Widen, strengthen, and enforce consultation and notification processes currently in place at the WTO. The intention to impose an export restriction would have to be notified in advance of the action being applied and a "fast track" consultation process could be put in place to discuss whether the measure can be avoided and how. Consultation should be ongoing and regular with a view to ensuring that the measure, once in place, is removed at the earliest possible moment.

5.8 Suggestion for Future Research

The current study has analysed Food Security Programme during Disaster and its Problems and Challenges in the case of Afar Region, Dewe district, Ethiopia. In regards to the response mechanisms employed by households, the current study has focused only on short term adjustments to food security problem. The long term adjustments in the mix of methods of securing food or income needed for obtaining food is not the focus of the current study. That is, though adaptive capacity has been included as one of the variables in the resilience analysis, adaptive strategies have not been explored in detail. Hence, exploring the adaptive strategies in the study area context in detail is another area that the future research can focus.

References

African Development Bank (2014). "Africa Food Security Brief: Special focus on climate Africa Food Security change Impacts". Statistics Department, Issue No 5, April 2014.

Anderson *et al.,* (2015). "*USAID Office of Food for Peace Food Security Country Framework for Ethiopia FY 2016 – FY 2020*". Washington, D.C.

Alinovi, L., D'Errico, M., Mane, E., & Romano, D. (2010). Livelihoods strategies and household resilience to food insecurity: An empirical analysis to Kenya. In conference organised by the European Report of Development, Dakar, Senegal, June (pp. 28-30).

Alinovi, L., Mane, E., and Romano, D. (2008). Towards the measurement of household resilience to food insecurity: applying a model to Palestinian household data. Sibrian R. (ed.), Deriving Food Security Information From National Household Budget Surveys, 137-52.

Burchi, F. and De Muro, P. (2012). A Human Development and Capability Approach to Food Security: Conceptual Framework and Informational Basis: WP 2012-009: February 2012, for UNDP Regional Bureau for Africa.

Creswell, J.W. (2009). Research Design Qualitative, Quantitative, and Mixed Methods Approaches, SAGE Publications, Inc.

Ciani, F. and Romano, D. (2013). Testing for household resilience to food insecurity: Evidence from Nicaragua.

Constas, M., and Barrett, C. B. (2013). Principles of resilience measurement for food insecurity: metrics, mechanisms, and implementation plans. Expert Consultation on Resilience Measurement Related to Food Security, Food and Agricultural Organisation and World Food Programme, Rome, Italy.

Census (2007). Afar Region Archived November 13, 2012, at the Wayback.

CSA (2007). Population and housing census of Ethiopia report for SNNPR. Available at: http://phe-ethiopia.org/pdf/snnpr.pdf.

CSA (2013). "Population Projection of Ethiopia for All Regions at Woreda Level from 2014 – 2017". Addis Ababa. Ethiopia.

Degefa (2009). An Assessment of the Role of Local Institutions and Social Capital in Household.

Food Security: A Case Study at Two Rural Communities in Oromiya Zone, Amhara region Degefa Tolossa (2005). Rural Livelihoods, Poverty, and Food insecurity in Ethiopia: A case study at Erenssa and Garbi Communities in Oromia Zone, Amhara National Regional State.

Doctorial Thesis for the degree of Philosofiae, Trondeim, May 2005.

Degefa Tolossa (2001). Causes of seasonal food insecurity in Oromia zone of the Amhara region: farmers' view. Department of Geography, Norwegian University of Science and Technology. Available at:wmich.edu/~asefa/.../Papers/2001 percent20papers/PaperI19.pdf

Desalegn Rahmato (2008). Ethiopia: Agriculture Policy Review. In Digest of Ethiopia's National Policies, Strategies, and Programmes, ed. Taye Assefa, Forum for Social Studies. Devereux, S. (2000). Food Insecurity in Ethiopia: A discussion paper for DFID.

Dibaba, D. B. and A. M. (2018). *Assessment on the Operationalisation of DRR System at Local Level.*

Dula Etana and Degefa Tolossa (2017).Unemployment and Food Insecurity in Urban Ethiopia. African Development Review, Vol. 29, No. 1, 2017, 56–68.

FAO (2016). The future of food and agriculture – Trends and challenges. Rome.

FAO, IFAD and WFP (2015). The State of Food Insecurity in the World 2015. Meeting the 2015 international hunger targets: taking stock of uneven progress. Rome, FAO.

FAO (2000). The state of food insecurity in the world. Food and Agriculture Organisation of the United Nations.

Field, A. (2005). Discovering statistics using SPSS. Second edition, SAGE Publications Fisseha Endale and Degefa Tolossa (2017). Food Security Status of People with Disabilities in Selassie *Kebele,* Hawassa Town, Southern Ethiopia. EJOSSAH, Vol. XIII, No.1, June 2017.

Fisseha, K., (2014), "Food insecurity and the relative importance of various household assets. The case of farm households in Southern Ethiopia". MSc Thesis, Swedish University Agricultural Sciences. [Accessed on January 29, 2015].

Frankenberger, T., Langworthy, M., Spangler, T., and Nelson, S. (2012). Enhancing Resilience to Food Security Shocks. TANGO International Inc.

Frankenberger, T. and Nelson, S. (2013). Background Paper for the Expert Consultation on Resilience Measurement for Food Security, paper presented at the expert Consultation on resilience measurement related to Food Security, 19–21 February 2013. Rome: FAO and WFP.

Frankenberger, T. (1992). Household food security: a conceptual review. In Maxwell, S. and Frankenberger T. (1992) (Eds). Household food security: concepts, indicators, measurements: A Technical Review. New York and Rome: UNICEF and IFAD.

Getn*et al*emu (2007). Revisiting the entitlement approach to famine: taking a closer look at the supply factor – a critical survey of the literature. Organisation for Social Science Research in Eastern and Southern Africa (OSSREA) V. XXIII, No. 2. Addis Ababa, Ethiopia.

Goitom Sisay (2017). Food Security Status of Peri-Urban Modern Small Scale Irrigation Project Beneficiary Female Headed Households in Kobo Town, Ethiopia. Journal of Food Security, 2017, Vol. 5, No. 6, 259-272. Available online at http://pubs.sciepub.com/jfs/5/6/6

Hailu, Ejara (2011). Baseline Survey of 55 Weredas of PCDP Phase II, Part I Archived July 20, at the Wayback Machine (Addis Ababa: August 2008), Annex 1 (accessed 23 March 2009) HailuEjaraKene, Baseline Survey, Annexes 16, 17 Machine.

Hoddinott, J. and Yisehac, Y. (2002). 'Dietary Diversity as a Food Security Indicator' FCND Discussion Paper, 136, IFPRI.

Israel, G. (2013). Determining Sample Size. University of Florida/ Institute of Food and Agricultural Sciences (IFAS).

LIFT and USAID (2011). Livelihood and food security conceptual framework. Livelihood and Food Security Technical Assistance (LFIT), FHI 360, Washington, DC 20009. Available @: marketshareassociates.com/wp.../LIFT-ES-Framework_8-17-2011.pd

Maxwell, D., Vaitla, B., Girmay, T. Nigussie, A. (2013). Resilience, Food Security Dynamics, and Poverty Traps in Northern Ethiopia Analysis of a Biannual Panel Dataset, 2011–2013.

Maxwell, D., Coates, J., and Vaitla, B. (2013). How Do Different Indicators of Household Food Security Compare? Empirical Evidence from Tigray. Feinstein International Center, Tufts University.

Maxwell, D. and Caldwell, R. (2008). The Coping Strategies Index: Field Methods Manual Second Edition.

Meseret, Meskele (2013). Determinants of household food insecurity status in Humbo *Wereda*, Wolayita, SNNPRS, ETHIOPIA. A Thesis submitted to the College of Agriculture Department of Rural Development and Agricultural Extension, School of Graduate Studies, Haramaya University.

Messay, Mulugeta (2015). Food Reserve System in Ethiopia: Assessment of the Current Implementation Technicalities and Policy Recommendations. Journal of Ethiopian Civil Society Organisations Volume III: An Annual Journal Published by the Consortium of Christian Relief and Development Association (CCRDA), Addis Ababa, 2015.

MoARD (2009). "Ethiopian Food security Programme (2010- 2014) ". Final August 2009.

Mulat, Demeke and Nigussie Tefera (2013). Sustainable resilience for food and nutrition security: The case of farming rural households in Ethiopia.

Mulugeta Tefera (2014). Resilience to drought induced food insecurity shocks: The case of Borena pastoral communities in Dire and Yabello Districts, Oromia, Ethiopia. A thesis submitted to the Center for Food Security Studies College of Development Studies.

Nigatu Regassa (2011). Small holder farmers coping strategies to household food insecurity and UNICEF (2014), "Ethiopia humanitarian situation report". htt://www.unicef.org/Ethiopia/

UNICEF_Ethiopia_SitRep_3_ May_and_June_2014_pdf hunger in Southern Ethiopia. Ethiopian Journal of Environmental Studies and Management, Vol. 4, No. 1, 2011.

Wiesmann, D., Bassett L., Benson T. and Hoddinott, J. (2008). Validation of Food Frequency and Dietary Diversity as Proxy Indicators of Household Food Security, report submitted to World Food Programmeme, Rome, by IFPRI.

Index